COLLINS

Student Support Materials for
Edexcel

AS BIOLOGY

Unit 3: **Energy and
the Environment**

Mary Jones
Geoff Jones

This booklet has been designed to support the Edexcel Biology AS specification. It contains some material which has been added in order to clarify the specification. The examination will be limited to material set out in the specification document.

Published by HarperCollins*Publishers* Limited
77–85 Fulham Palace Road
Hammersmith
London
W6 8JB

Browse the complete Collins catalogue at
www.collinseducation.com

First published 2000, Reprinted 2001, 2002, 2004 (twice), 2005

10 9 8
ISBN-13 978 0 00 327714 2
ISBN-10 0 00 327714 3

Mary Jones and Geoff Jones assert the moral right to be identified as the authors of this work

British Library Cataloguing in Publication Data
A catalogue record for this publication is available from the British Library

Cover designed by Chi Leung
Editorial, design and production by Gecko Limited, Cambridge
Printed in Hong Kong by Printing Express Ltd.

The publisher wishes to thank the Edexcel Foundation for permission to reproduce the examination questions.

You might also like to visit:
www.harpercollins.com
The book lover's website

Other useful texts

Full colour textbooks
Collins Advanced Science: Biology
Collins Advanced Science: Human Biology

Student Support Booklets
Edexcel Biology: 1 Molecules and Cells
Edexcel Biology: 2 Exchange, Transport and Reproduction

What books do I need to study this course?

You will probably use a range of resources during your course. Some will be produced by the centre where you are studying, some by a commercial publisher and others may be borrowed from libraries or study centres. Different resources have different uses – but remember, owning a book is not enough – it must be *used*.

What does this booklet cover?

This *Student Support Booklet* covers the content you need to know and understand to pass the unit test for Edexcel Biology AS Unit 3: Energy and the Environment. It is very concise and you will need to study it carefully to make sure you can remember all of the material.

How can I remember all this material?

Reading the booklet is an essential first step – but reading by itself is not a good way to get stuff into your memory. If you have bought the booklet and can write on it, you could try the following techniques to help you to memorise the material:

- underline or highlight the most important words in every paragraph
- underline or highlight scientific jargon – write a note of the meaning in the margin if you are unsure
- remember the number of items in a list – then you can tell if you have forgotten one when you try to remember it later
- tick sections when you are sure you know them – and then concentrate on the sections you do not yet know.

How can I check my progress?

The unit test at the end is a useful check on your progress – you may want to wait until you have nearly completed the unit and use it as a mock exam or try questions one by one as you progress. The answers show you how much you need to do to get the marks.

What if I get stuck?

A colour textbook such as *Collins Advanced Science: Biology* provides more explanation than this booklet. It may help you to make progress if you get stuck.

Any other good advice?

- You will not learn well if you are tired or stressed. Set aside time for work (and play!) and try to stick to it.
- Don't leave everything until the last minute – whatever your friends may tell you it doesn't work.
- You are most effective if you work hard for shorter periods of time and then take a (short!) break. 30 minutes of work followed by a five or ten minute break is a useful pattern. Then get back to work.
- Some people work better in the morning, some in the evening. Find out which works better for you and do that whenever possible.
- Do not suffer in silence – ask friends and your teacher for help.
- Stay calm, enjoy it and … good luck!

Further explanation references give a little extra detail, or direct you to other texts if you need more help or need to read around a topic.

The main text gives a very concise explanation of the ideas in your course. You must study all of it – none is spare or not needed.

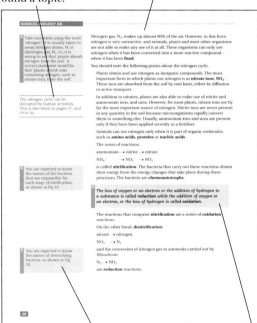

The examiner's notes are always useful – make sure you read them because they will help with your module test.

There are rigorous definitions of the main terms used in your examination – memorise these exactly.

1 Modes of nutrition

Living organisms require various substances from their environment, which they use as:

- sources of atoms and molecules for building their bodies
- sources of chemical potential energy, which they can convert to other types of energy to maintain life.

These substances are called **nutrients**. Taking in nutrients from the environment is called **nutrition**.

Autotrophic and heterotrophic nutrition

The nutrients that organisms take in may be **inorganic** or **organic**.

 *An **inorganic** substance is usually one in which the molecules or ions are relatively small, and which does not contain carbon.*

Water, oxygen, nitrate ions and carbon dioxide are all examples of inorganic substances – carbon dioxide qualifies because it has small molecules, even though it contains carbon.

 *An **organic** substance is usually one in which the molecules are relatively large, and which contains carbon.*

Glucose and all other carbohydrates, amino acids and proteins, lipids, nucleotides and vitamins are examples of organic substances.

 *Some organisms need to take in only inorganic nutrients. These organisms are called **autotrophs**.*

Plants are autotrophs. They take in water, carbon dioxide and various mineral ions, and use these to make all the organic molecules that they need. Their source of energy is sunlight. They do not need any other energy source. Plants are able to transfer the energy from sunlight into chemical potential energy, which is stored in the organic molecules that they make.

 *Some organisms require a mix of organic and inorganic nutrients. These organisms are called **heterotrophs**.*

All animals, including humans, are heterotrophs. We need to take in a wide range of organic substances, including carbohydrates, proteins, lipids and vitamins, as well as some inorganic ones, namely various mineral ions and water. Our source of energy is the chemical potential energy in the organic molecules that we eat.

Heterotrophs, therefore, depend on a supply of organic substances that have been made by autotrophs, both as a source of the molecules from which their bodies are made, and as a source of energy.

Holozoic nutrition

Holozoic nutrition is a type of heterotrophic nutrition. In holozoic nutrition, the organism feeds by taking nutrients into its body, usually into some form of gut or **alimentary canal**. The nutrients come from other organisms' bodies. The organic molecules are broken down – **hydrolysed** or digested – inside the alimentary canal, and then **absorbed** through the wall of the canal and into the organism's body. This is how humans feed.

Herbivores

Some holozoic organisms feed entirely on material from the bodies of plants. They are called **herbivores**. Much of a plant's body is made up of the polysaccharide **cellulose**, which is difficult to digest. Cellulose molecules are long chains of glucose molecules joined with β(1-4) links. Most animals are not able to produce the enzyme cellulase which catalyses the hydrolysis of these links, so they cannot digest cellulose. If a herbivore does not digest the cellulose in the plant material that it eats, it is missing out on an enormous amount of chemical potential energy. Moreover, the cells of the plant – containing all sorts of other useful nutrients – are surrounded by cellulose cell walls. If these are not broken down, most of the cell contents will not be digested and absorbed.

Herbivores have evolved specialised alimentary canals that help them to digest cellulose. **Ruminants**, such as cattle and sheep, are excellent examples of animals with a gut that is adapted for the digestion of cellulose.

Figs 1 a and b on page 6 show the jaws and teeth of a cow. Most of the teeth are **molars** and **premolars**. They are large, broad teeth with ridges and grooves on their surfaces. The ridges of the bottom teeth fit into the grooves in the top teeth, and vice versa. As the cow chews, the lower jaw moves from side to side, so the teeth grind against each other, crushing the food between them. This helps to break up the plant material, and can even begin to break the cell walls apart, providing a larger surface area for enzymes to work on after the food is swallowed.

In front of the molars and premolars, there is a gap where no teeth are present, called the **diastema**. If you get a chance to watch a cow chewing, you will see that it uses this space to allow its large, muscular tongue to manipulate the grass in its mouth, turning it so that it can be chewed from all angles.

The teeth at the front of the mouth are present only in the bottom jaw; the top jaw just has a hard, horny pad. The teeth are called **incisors** and

Premolars and molars have very similar structures. Premolars are nearer the front of the mouth than molars. The other difference between them is that premolars are present both in the milk teeth (the first set of teeth that mammals have when young) and in the adult teeth. Molars only appear in the adult set of teeth.

canines. They have surfaces shaped like the end of a chisel and are used to crop mouthfuls of plants such as grass, cutting it against the pad on the upper jaw.

Fig 1
(a) Side view of the jaws of a cow
(b) A cow's molar tooth

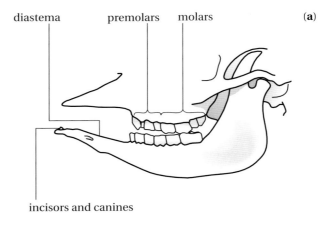

diastema   premolars   molars   **(a)**

incisors and canines

(b)

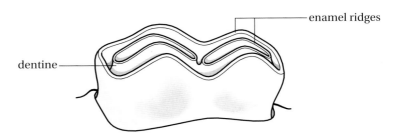

enamel ridges

dentine

Fig 2 shows the structure of a cow's stomach. It has four chambers. Chewed food passes first into the **reticulum** and then into the **rumen**. There are huge numbers of microorganisms living in the anaerobic conditions of both of these chambers. Many of the microbes secrete cellulase which breaks down cellulose. The product of this breakdown is glucose, but the microorganisms convert the glucose to fatty acids, carbon dioxide and methane. The fatty acids are absorbed through the walls of the rumen and into the cow's bloodstream.

Cattle produce enormous quantities of carbon dioxide and methane. This passes up their oesophagus and into the air. The gases produced by ruminants are thought to make a significant contribution to the enhanced greenhouse effect and, therefore, to global warming.

To increase the efficiency with which plant material is broken down, some of the semi-digested material in the rumen and reticulum periodically passes back up the oesophagus into the cow's mouth, where it is chewed all over again ('chewing the cud'). It is then re-swallowed so that more of the cellulose in it can be digested.

From the rumen, the partly digested food passes into the **omasum** and **abomasum**. The abomasum is the equivalent of the stomach in humans, and – as in humans – it secretes **proteases** that hydrolyse proteins, converting them to polypeptides and eventually to amino acids. These proteins may have come directly from the grass that the cow has eaten.

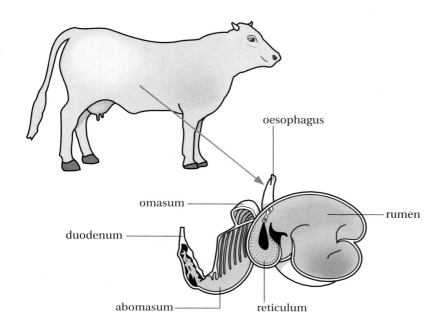

Fig 2
The structure of a cow's stomach

The cow also gets a large quantity of protein from the microorganisms that live in the rumen and reticulum and which are themselves digested.

The relationship between the cow and the microorganisms inside its rumen and reticulum is one from which both partners benefit. The cow gets cellulose digested for it, and also gets proteins from the digestion of the microorganisms. The microorganisms get a constant supply of food, in an environment that is warm and moist and, therefore, conducive to rapid growth and multiplication (even though many of them are eventually digested). Such a relationship is known as **mutualism** and another example is described on page 10.

Carnivores

A holozoic organism that feeds almost entirely on the bodies of animals is known as a **carnivore**. Many carnivores kill and eat live prey; they are called **predators**. Others eat meat from animals that have previously died; they are called **scavengers**.

Cats are predatory carnivores. Figs 3 a and b on page 8 show the jaws and teeth of a cat. The most obvious teeth are the large, pointed **canines**. These long, sharp teeth are used for piercing and killing prey. In front of these are the **incisors**, which are much smaller than the cow's and which are used mainly for nibbling pieces of meat from bones, and also for cleaning the animal's own fur.

The **molars** and **premolars**, in complete contrast to the cow's teeth, look like a mountain range with a sharp ridge all along the top. The top teeth cut *past* the bottom ones (remember that the cow's bottom molars grind from side to side *against* the upper ones). The cat's teeth, therefore, act like scissor blades, chopping through flesh and bone like shears. The jaws move crisply up and down when a cat chews, not from side to side as in a cow.

Fig 3
(a) Side view of a cat's skull
(b) A cat's molar tooth

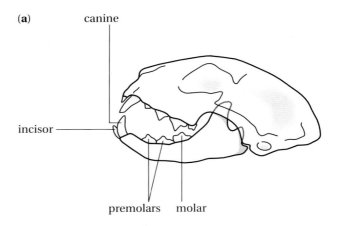

(a)

canine

incisor

premolars   molar

(b)

Cats and most other predators tend not to chew their food much – often they just bite it into pieces small enough to swallow and then gulp it down. They can afford to do this because the cells in the animal material that they eat do not contain cellulose, and so are easy to digest. It does not matter if the material remains in pieces because, when it reaches the stomach, the hydrochloric acid and protease enzymes produced here will break it down quickly. Moreover, predators often eat in situations in which, if they do not eat as much and as quickly as possible, some other predator or scavenger may steal its kill. There's no time for chewing!

Saprobiontic and parasitic nutrition

Both saprobiontic and parasitic nutrition are types of heterotrophic nutrition.

Saprobionts, sometimes known as **saprotrophs** or **saprophytes**, are organisms that feed by secreting digestive enzymes onto the organic materials on which they live. These materials are called **substrates**. They are often derived from dead animals or plants, including substances like dead wood, leather, animal faeces, and human food materials, such as bread.

Many saprobionts can feed on living organisms as well as dead ones, or on non-living material derived from living tissue. Similarly, many parasites (see page 9) may continue to feed on their host after it is dead. It is, therefore, not always possible to draw a sharp dividing line between saprobiontic nutrition and parasitic nutrition.

The fungus *Rhizopus* is an example of a saprobiont (Fig 4). Like all fungi, it feeds by secreting enzymes from its hyphae into the substrate on which it is living. This may be a living plant – such as wheat – or agar jelly in a Petri dish. The enzymes hydrolyse large organic molecules such as polysaccharides and proteins in the substrate, and convert them to small soluble molecules such as sugars and amino acids. These molecules are then absorbed into the hyphae by diffusion and active transport.

The singular of hyphae is hypha.

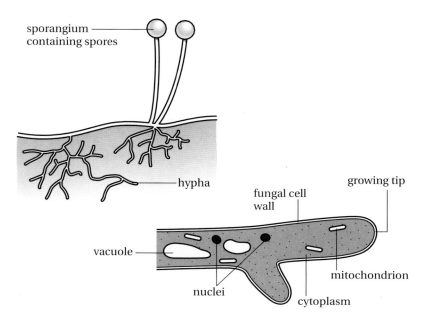

Fig 4
Rhizopus

The mycelium is the collection of hyphae belonging to one individual.

Parasites are organisms that live on and feed from another living organism of a different species, called the **host**. The parasite benefits from the relationship, but the host does not. An example of a parasite is the human tapeworm *Taenia solium*. Like many parasites, it has different hosts at different stages of its life cycle. *Taenia* lives in the human alimentary canal as an adult, but also spends some of the early stages of its life history in pigs. Humans can, therefore, become infected with this tapeworm by eating infected and undercooked pork.

Fig 5 shows the structure of an adult *Taenia solium*. It lives surrounded by food material that has already been digested by its host's enzymes. *Taenia*, therefore, has no alimentary canal at all, but simply absorbs digested food through its body wall.

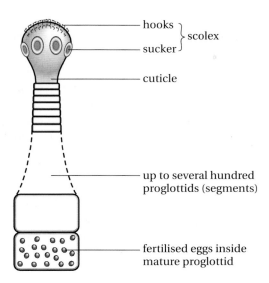

Fig 5
Structure of *Taenia solium*

Living inside another organism poses considerable problems. Tapeworms have evolved a number of adaptations that allow them to survive in these difficult conditions.

- The tapeworm has an array of hooks and suckers on its **scolex**. These anchor it firmly in position and prevent it from being pushed along and out of the alimentary canal by peristaltic movements.

- It has a protective, non-living covering or **cuticle** that prevents the gut's hydrolytic enzymes from digesting its body surface.

- Respiration is anaerobic, as there is no oxygen inside the alimentary canal.

- The chances of a tapeworm's offspring reaching a new human host are very small, so enormous numbers are produced. Reproduction is sexual. Although each tapeworm is **hermaphrodite** (meaning that it produces both eggs and sperms), they do not normally self-fertilise but mate with another tapeworm. Huge quantities of fertilised eggs are produced inside several hundred **proglottids**, which break off and pass out of the host's alimentary canal through the anus. Most of these eggs die, but there is a chance that some may be eaten by a pig. If so, they develop inside the pig. The tapeworm then has a chance of infecting a human host if a person eats undercooked meat from this pig.

Mutualistic nutrition

Mutualism is the term used to describe a relationship between two organisms of different species, which live in very close association with one another. Both organisms benefit from this relationship. If the benefit gained by both is in terms of nutrition, then the relationship can be termed mutualistic nutrition.

One example of mutualistic nutrition – that between cattle and their cellulose-digesting microorganisms – has been described on pages 6 and 7. Another example is the relationship between the nitrogen-fixing bacterium *Rhizobium* and plants belonging to the family Papilionaceae. This family includes peas and beans.

All plants require nitrogen atoms, which they use to make amino acids and proteins. As you will see on page 20, plants can only use these atoms if they are part of some compound, such as nitrate ions or ammonium ions. The bacterium *Rhizobium* is able to use nitrogen gas, N_2, from the air and convert it to ammonia, NH_3. This process is called **nitrogen fixation**.

Rhizobium lives in very close association with the host plant. As the young seedling grows, *Rhizobium* in the soil invades its roots, which stimulates the roots to grow **nodules**. The bacteria live inside the plant cells in these nodules. They synthesise an enzyme called **nitrogenase**, which catalyses the conversion of nitrogen gas – obtained from the air in the spaces between the soil particles – to ammonia. This requires a large input of energy, which is supplied from the energy-rich carbon compounds that the plant makes in photosynthesis.

E | Take care not to confuse *Rhizopus* and *Rhizobium*.

The ammonia that the *Rhizobium* makes is converted to amino acids, which are transported to other parts of the plant through the xylem vessels.

You can see that both organisms benefit from the relationship. *Rhizobium* has a place to live and a supply of energy-rich carbon compounds. The plant gains a good supply of amino acids. Plants with *Rhizobium* in their roots are able to grow well, even on soils where nitrates are in very short supply.

2   Ecosystems

Ecology is the study of living organisms in their environment. Ecology is a very broad subject, and ecologists use a variety of terms that have precise meanings within this subject area.

A **population** is a group of organisms of the same species that live in the same area at the same time, and – if sexually reproducing – can interbreed with each other. All the populations, of all the different species, living in an area at one time make up a **community**. The place where an organism, a species, a population or a community lives is called a **habitat**.

The community that lives in an area, plus all the non-living parts of that area, together make up an **ecosystem**. Thus, an oak wood can be considered to be an ecosystem. The oak wood ecosystem includes all the living things in the wood, plus the soil, rocks, pools of water and the air around them. You can think of ecosystems on any scale. So, inside the oak wood, you could consider a rotten crab apple with a community of fungi living on it, to be a miniature ecosystem. On a broader scale, some ecologists consider the whole Earth to be one huge ecosystem, called the **biosphere**.

All living organisms need a supply of energy. Energy enters almost all ecosystems as **sunlight**. Plants and some photosynthetic bacteria transfer energy from sunlight into chemical potential energy in organic compounds such as carbohydrates. They are called **producers**. All the other organisms in the ecosystem obtain their energy by feeding, either directly or indirectly, on the energy-containing compounds made by the plants. They are called **consumers**.

The pathway through which energy is transferred between the organisms in the ecosystem can be shown diagrammatically as a **food chain** or **food web** (Fig 6). The arrows in a food chain or food web indicate the direction of energy transfer.

The position in a food web at which an organism feeds is called a **trophic level**. The first trophic level includes the producers (plants), and the second includes **herbivores** (animals that eat plants). Animals that eat other animals are called **carnivores**. Many animals feed at more than one trophic level. For example, although foxes are mostly carnivores, they also eat significant amounts of fruits such as blackberries.

An extremely important group of organisms in any ecosystem is the **decomposers**. These are organisms that feed on dead bodies and waste from all the other organisms in the ecosystem. They are, therefore, often omitted from diagrams of food webs, because there would be arrows leading from absolutely every organism in the web to the decomposers, which would make the web look very confusing. Decomposers are, of course, consumers. As you will see on pages 18, decomposers are crucial in the recycling of materials such as carbon and nitrogen through an ecosystem.

E Many of the terms used in ecology are words that also have less precise or slightly different meanings in everyday use. Take care to learn their precise meanings within ecology, and use them carefully in your examination answers.

Not all ecosystems rely on sunlight as their fundamental source of energy. For example, in a number of areas deep under the oceans, hot solutions of various chemicals flow upwards from beneath the Earth's crust. Microorganisms are able to use these as a source of energy, and complex ecosystems including large worms, crabs and fish are based on this unusual energy source.

Fig 6
A food chain and a food web

Food chain

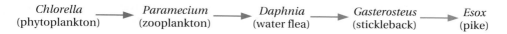

Food web

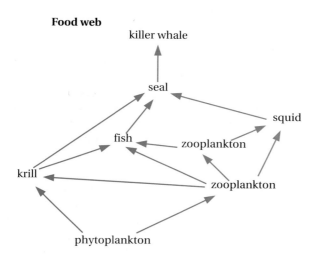

3 Energy flow

You have seen that energy enters most ecosystems as sunlight, and that this energy is transferred to energy in organic compounds by producers such as green plants. This is done by **photosynthesis**. Photosynthesis takes place inside **chloroplasts**, which are found mostly in the palisade and spongy mesophyll cells in plant leaves. Light energy of certain wavelengths (especially red and blue light) is absorbed by the green pigment **chlorophyll**, and this energy drives the reactions that result in the combination of carbon dioxide and water to form carbohydrates. The reactions involved are complex, as you will see if you continue your studies to A2, but they can be summarised in a simple equation:

$$6CO_2 + 6H_2O \rightarrow C_6H_{12}O_6 + 6O_2$$

In this process, some of the light energy is transferred to chemical potential energy in the molecules of carbohydrate. However, much of the light energy that enters the ecosystem is *not* transferred to carbohydrate, because:

- a lot of light does not hit the plant leaves at all and even the light which hits the leaves may be reflected from the surface, or may pass in but not hit a chlorophyll molecule in a chloroplast – it just passes straight through the leaf
- chlorophyll can only absorb light of certain wavelengths, so the other wavelengths pass straight through the leaf
- whenever energy is transferred from one form to another, some is lost as heat. This happens in the reactions of photosynthesis, so not all of the energy absorbed by the chlorophyll is transferred to energy in carbohydrate molecules.

Herbivores feed on plants, thus obtaining energy from the carbohydrate and other organic molecules that the plants contain. Once again, however, energy is lost, as not all the energy that the plant transferred into carbohydrates is transferred to the herbivore. This is because:

- the plant itself breaks down some of its energy-containing carbohydrates to supply energy for its own metabolic processes, such as active transport – it does this by respiration, converting the carbohydrates to carbon dioxide and water
- not all of the plants and not all parts of each plant are eaten, for example, many herbivores eat only leaves, not roots
- not all of the plant material that is eaten by the herbivore is digested and absorbed into its body – undigested material passes straight through the alimentary canal and leaves the body as faeces.

The loss of energy continues at each step of a food chain.

Pyramids of numbers, biomass and energy

A pyramid of numbers (or biomass or energy) is a graphical representation of the numbers or biomass of organisms at each trophic level in a food web, or of the energy contained within them (Fig 7). The area of each box represents the number, mass or energy content of the organisms at that trophic level.

Fig 7
Ecological pyramid diagrams

Pyramids of numbers

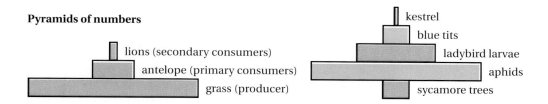

Pyramid of biomass

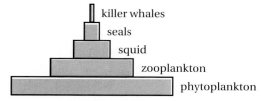

Pyramid of energy

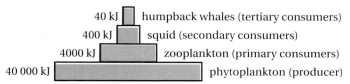

You have seen that energy is lost as it passes from organism to organism along a food chain. Thus, the further you move along a food chain, the greater the proportion of the original energy that has been lost to the environment as heat. Organisms that feed at higher trophic levels have less energy available to them than organisms feeding at lower trophic levels. As less energy is available, less living material can be supported. So the producers in an ecosystem usually account for more living material (biomass) than the consumers. A **pyramid of biomass** shows this clearly.

The biomass may be **wet mass**, which is simply the mass of the living organisms. Alternatively, it may be measured as **dry mass**, which is their mass after all water has been driven off.

Wet mass is much easier to measure than dry mass, but dry mass is more informative as organisms vary greatly in the proportion of their body mass that is made up of water.

Pyramids of numbers are not always very informative, because they do not take the size of the organisms into account. For example, the sycamore trees in the second pyramid in Fig 7 have a smaller box than the huge numbers of tiny aphids feeding on them.

Pyramids of energy, on the other hand, are even more informative than pyramids of biomass. The amount of chemical potential energy that is contained within a certain mass of each kind of organism is found, and then this is multiplied by the total biomass of those organisms. This method is, therefore, the most accurate for indicating the way in which *energy* is transferred up through the trophic levels, as it takes into account the differences in energy content of different kinds of organisms.

Productivity

> **Productivity** *can be defined as the amount of energy incorporated into the organisms in a trophic level over a given period of time.*

Productivity is calculated for a given area, usually one square metre, over a certain period of time, usually one year. So, productivity is usually measured in units of kilojoules per m² per year, that is $kJ\ m^{-2}\ y^{-1}$.

Productivity can be measured for organisms at any trophic level. If it is done for the producers (plants), then it is called **primary productivity**.

Gross primary production is the rate at which the producers transfer light energy into energy in their organic molecules. It is a measure of the amount of new organic compounds that plants make in photosynthesis. However, as you have seen, plants break down some of these compounds by respiration, releasing the energy from them and using it for themselves. The amount of energy available to the consumers, therefore, is what is left *after* the plants have used some, i.e. the gross primary production minus the energy that the plants use. This is called **net primary production**.

Net primary production is sometimes abbreviated to NPP, and gross primary production to GPP.

net primary production = gross primary production − respiration

4 Recycling of nutrients

The atoms, ions and molecules that organisms need to form their cells are passed from one organism to another, and between the organisms and their environment. One example of this recycling is the **water cycle** (Fig 8).

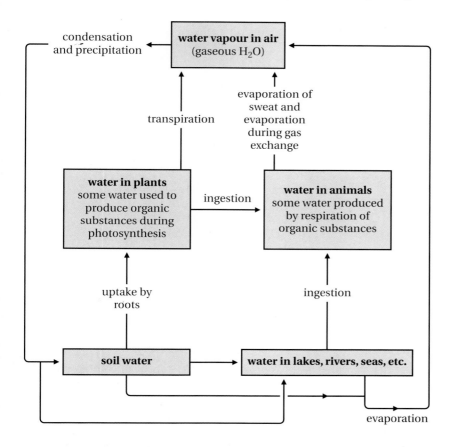

Fig 8
The water cycle

The carbon cycle

All organic molecules contain carbon. Living organisms, therefore, contain carbon atoms in carbohydrates, proteins, lipids, nucleic acids and other molecules in their bodies. Fig 9 on page 18 shows how carbon atoms are cycled between the air, living organisms, the sea and rocks.

The air contains carbon atoms in the compound **carbon dioxide**. Some of this dissolves in water, where a proportion of it reacts with the water to form **hydrogencarbonate** ions, HCO_3^-. Plants and some microorganisms can use either carbon dioxide or hydrogencarbonate ions in photosynthesis, so that the carbon atoms become part of the organic molecules in their cells.

These organic molecules may be passed on to other living organisms which feed on the plants. They may be broken down in respiration, in which case the carbon in them is re-converted to carbon dioxide and returned to the air or water.

Fig 9
The carbon cycle

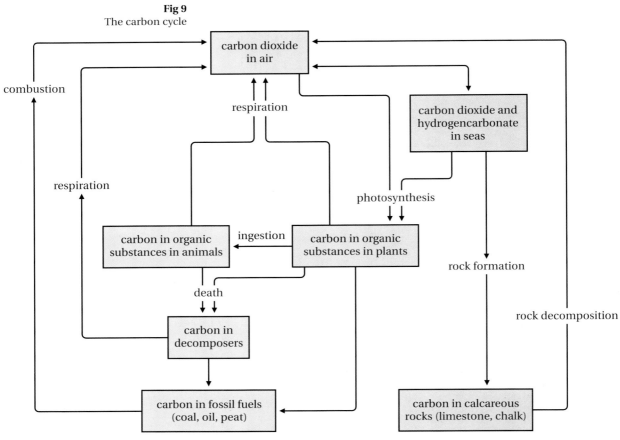

Dead organisms may be broken down fairly quickly by microorganisms and other decomposers, which again use the organic compounds in respiration and release carbon dioxide. Sometimes, though, especially in anaerobic environments such as bogs, dead bodies do not decompose completely but become part of the soil. When present in high concentrations, they form substances such as peat, coal or oil. World wide, these substances contain very large amounts of carbon.

In the sea, many tiny organisms use hydrogencarbonate ions, together with calcium ions, to make their shells. These shells are constructed from **calcium carbonate**. As the organisms die, their shells fall to the bottom of the sea, where they accumulate over many years to form **limestone** rocks. Eventually, tectonic movements may cause these rocks to be taken deep below the Earth's surface, where they melt and may rise to the surface as **magma** during volcanic eruptions. Carbon dioxide is released from volcanoes, and so the carbon returns to the atmosphere once more. Carbon dioxide is also released from exposed limestone as a result of weathering.

We still do not know exactly how much carbon is present in all of the different places described above. It is probable that most carbon is locked up in rocks, which can be thought of as a long-term store or **sink** for carbon. The next largest store for carbon is the seas and oceans, where the water and sediments probably contain about 55 times as much carbon as the atmosphere. Next come soils on land, which contain about twice as much carbon as the atmosphere.

Plants probably contain about the same amount of carbon as the atmosphere. However, most ecologists do not consider that plants are really sinks for carbon, because the total activity of all the plants on Earth results in just as much carbon released in respiration as taken in for photosynthesis.

The carbon cycle can be disrupted by human activities. This is described on pages 25 to 27.

The nitrogen cycle

Living organisms require nitrogen because nitrogen atoms are contained in proteins and nucleic acids. Fig 10 shows how nitrogen atoms are cycled between living organisms and their environment.

Fig 10
The nitrogen cycle

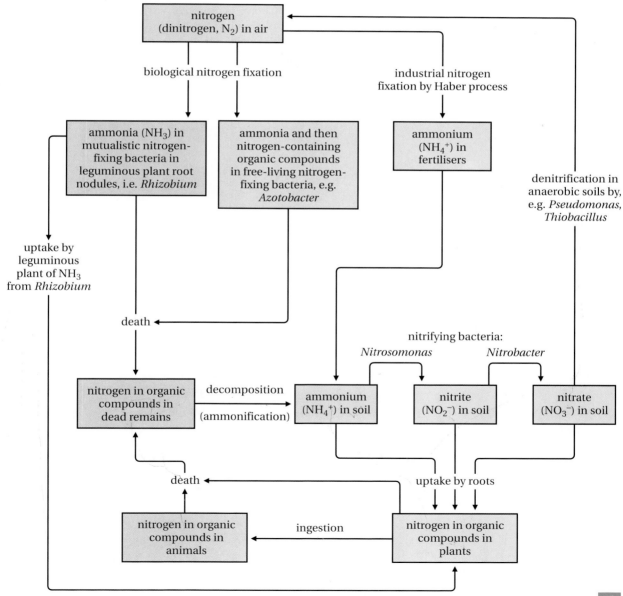

E Take care when using the word 'nitrogen'. It is usually taken to mean nitrogen atoms, N, or dinitrogen gas, N_2. So, it is wrong to say that 'plants absorb nitrogen from the soil'. A correct statement would be that 'plants absorb ions containing nitrogen, such as nitrate ions, from the soil'.

The nitrogen cycle can be disrupted by human activities. This is described on pages 27, and 30 to 31.

E You are expected to know the names of the bacteria that are responsible for each stage of nitrification, as shown in Fig 10.

E You are expected to know the names of denitrifying bacteria, as shown in Fig 10.

Nitrogen gas, N_2, makes up almost 80% of the air. However, in this form nitrogen is very unreactive, and animals, plants and most other organisms are not able to make any use of it at all. These organisms can only use nitrogen when it has been converted into a more reactive compound – when it has been **fixed**.

You should note the following points about the nitrogen cycle.

Plants obtain and use nitrogen as inorganic compounds. The most important form in which plants use nitrogen is as **nitrate ions, NO_3^-**. These ions are absorbed from the soil by root hairs, either by diffusion or active transport.

In addition to nitrates, plants are also able to make use of nitrite and ammonium ions, and urea. However, for most plants, nitrate ions are by far the most important source of nitrogen. Nitrite ions are never present in any quantity in the soil because microorganisms rapidly convert them to something else. Usually, ammonium ions and urea are present only if they have been applied recently as a fertiliser.

Animals can use nitrogen only when it is part of organic molecules, such as **amino acids**, **proteins** or **nucleic acids**.

The series of reactions:

ammonium → nitrite → nitrate

$NH_4^+ \quad \rightarrow NO_2^- \rightarrow NO_3^-$

is called **nitrification**. The bacteria that carry out these reactions obtain their energy from the energy changes that take place during these processes. The bacteria are **chemoautotrophs**.

D *The loss of oxygen or an electron, or the addition of hydrogen to a substance is called* **reduction**, *while the addition of oxygen or an electron, or the loss of hydrogen is called* **oxidation**.

The reactions that comprise **nitrification** are a series of **oxidation** reactions.

On the other hand, **denitrification**:

nitrate → nitrogen

$NO_3^- \quad \rightarrow N_2$

and the conversion of nitrogen gas to ammonia carried out by *Rhizobium*:

$N_2 \rightarrow NH_3$

are **reduction** reactions.

5 Energy resources

Apart from the energy contained in food, which we need to drive our
metabolic reactions, humans use enormous amounts of energy for other
purposes. For example, industries use energy to manufacture products, all
forms of transport use energy and we use energy to maintain our
environment at a suitable temperature. We obtain this energy from a wide
range of sources, some of which are **non-renewable** (that is, they are finite
and will eventually run out) and some which are **renewable** (that is, the
sources are constantly regenerated). Our use of energy can have a
considerable impact on living organisms – for example, the burning of
fossil fuels disrupts the carbon cycle and causes air pollution.

Over the long term, we need to ensure that our use of energy resources is
sustainable, which means that:

- we do not use up non-renewable energy resources so rapidly and so
  carelessly that there are none left for future generations (unless we are
  sure that there are ways in which the use of renewable resources can be
  increased to compensate)

- we do not do irreparable harm to the environment by the way in which
  we use energy resources, such as by causing pollution or by reducing
  biodiversity.

Fossil fuels

Examples of non-renewable energy sources are the **fossil fuels**. These are
fuels that were formed from living organisms, a very long time ago. Many
of them were formed 300 million years ago, in the Carboniferous period. At
this time, much of the world was covered with swamps, in which huge
quantities of semi-decayed plant material built up. Over time, these
remains became compressed to form coal. In a similar way,
microorganisms decayed to form oil and natural gas. All of these
substances contain large amounts of carbon, and large amounts of
chemical potential energy. When they burn, the carbon combines with
oxygen in the air to form carbon dioxide and water. The chemical potential
energy is transferred to heat energy, which we can use for heating (e.g. coal
fires in the home), to turn turbines that allow electricity to be generated
(e.g. in coal-fired or oil-burning power stations), or to produce movement
(e.g. when petrol, which is obtained from oil, is burned in a car engine).

There are several environmental and economic problems associated with
the use of fossil fuels:

- fossil fuels will eventually run out – there is not an unlimited supply

- the gases that are released when they burn cause pollution. All of them
  release carbon dioxide, which contributes to the enhanced greenhouse
  effect. This is described on page 28. Coal also produces sulphur dioxide,
  which causes acid rain. This is described on pages 27 and 28.

There is, therefore, an increasing interest in the use of alternative,
renewable sources of energy.

Renewable energy sources

Increasingly, a wide range of renewable energy sources is being used all around the world. Several of these involve living organisms, including:

- fast-growing biomass
- gasohol, obtained from sugar
- biogas, from domestic and agricultural wastes.

Fast-growing biomass means plant material obtained from fast-growing trees or other plants. Several types of plants are being used, for example willow trees in Britain and the giant grass *Miscanthus* in warmer parts of the world. They are harvested and burnt for fuel, for example in the home or on a large scale at power stations to generate electricity.

The advantages of using fast-growing biomass for fuel include the following.

> This is a renewable energy source. The plants absorb energy from sunlight and transfer it to chemical potential energy in their tissues. As the plants are harvested, more plants can be planted or the old ones regrown (see page 26).

> Although the biomass does release carbon dioxide when it is burnt, this is only as much as the carbon dioxide that was absorbed by the plants for photosynthesis. So the net balance for carbon dioxide uptake and output is zero. Thus, the growing and burning of fast-growing biomass does not contribute to the enhanced greenhouse effect.

The disadvantages include the following.

> The biomass does not contain large quantities of energy per kilogram, when compared with fuels such as coal or oil. Thus, very large areas must be planted to generate enough fuel to serve even a very small power station.

> This also means that transport costs are high, because a very large bulk of material is needed to supply a relatively modest amount of energy. For this reason, it is only economic to use fast-growing biomass close to the area where it is grown.

> Although the carbon dioxide balance for the plants themselves is zero, this does not take into account use of fuel for harvesting and trans-porting the biomass. So, overall, there is a net output of carbon dioxide.

Gasohol is another partly renewable energy source which is obtained from living organisms. Gasohol is a mixture of the non-renewable fossil fuel petrol, obtained from oil, and the renewable fuel ethanol, produced by the fermentation of a sugar-containing substance by the yeast *Saccharomyces*. For example, in Brazil, the fast-growing crop sugar cane has been used as a sugar source.

The advantages of using gasohol for fuel are the same as those of using fast-growing biomass. The main disadvantage is that producing ethanol from crops such as sugar cane is expensive; it involves high transport costs, and it is expensive to run the fermentation plants. It is only economic if the cost of fossil fuels is extremely high, as was the case in Brazil in the

1980s. However, now that Brazil can afford to import oil, it is cheaper to do this. Farmers get more money selling their sugar cane for the production of sugar, rather than gasohol.

Biogas is a mixture of **methane** and carbon dioxide that is produced from the fermentation of domestic and agricultural wastes. Chemical potential energy in biomass in these wastes is converted to chemical potential energy in methane by several different types of bacteria. The stages in this conversion are:

1 **aerobic bacteria** hydrolyse carbohydrates, proteins and lipids in the wastes to monosaccharides, amino acids, fatty acids and glycerol. Other bacteria then use these substances as substrates to form **short-chain fatty acids**, such as ethanoic (acetic) acid. Carbon dioxide is also produced during this stage.

2 after the aerobic bacteria have used up the oxygen, **anaerobic bacteria** convert the fatty acids to **methane**.

Fig 11 shows a **biogas digester** in which these conversions take place. Biogas digesters are often very simple in design, as they are frequently used in rural areas by individual families or small communities. The essential features are:

- the digester must be closed, so that anaerobic conditions are produced; otherwise, the anaerobic bacteria cannot produce methane

- the temperature is often maintained at between 30 °C and 40 °C – this can be helped by building the digester into the ground, which provides insulation

- there must be an easy way of adding waste to the digester, and an easy way of extracting the methane from it.

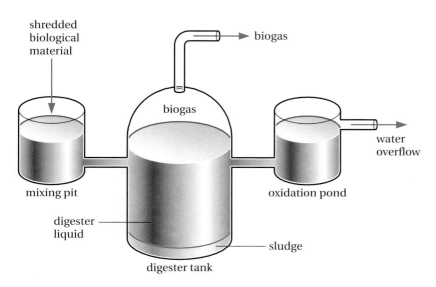

Fig 11
A biogas digester

Advantages of the use of biogas as a fuel include the following.

It is a renewable energy source; whenever plants are grown or animals farmed, waste is produced that can be used to generate fuel.

It is a very cheap source of fuel for rural, farming communities. There are no transport costs, because biogas can be made where it is needed. The raw materials are otherwise worthless waste products. It also solves the problem of how to dispose of these wastes.

When methane burns, it produces only water vapour and carbon dioxide. However the amount of carbon dioxide is no more than was originally absorbed by the plant material that makes up the waste. Thus, the net carbon dioxide change in the atmosphere is zero.

The disadvantage, as for fast-growing biomass, is the relatively low energy content of the waste which means that it is uneconomic to transport the material over long distances to, for example, a large power station. This limits its use to areas close to the production of the waste.

6 Human influences on the environment

Human activities have always affected the environment. As the human population has increased, and as the use of energy resources has increased, the effects of human activity have also increased. Harmful effects of humans on the environment include:

- direct damage to habitats as a result of **deforestation** and **desertification**

- pollution – that is, the addition of harmful substances to the environment. This includes **atmospheric pollution** (for example the production of acid rain, and enhancement of the greenhouse effect) and **water pollution** (for example, by raw sewage and fertilisers).

Deforestation

Deforestation is the removal of forests. If there were no humans present, the natural vegetation in many parts of the world would be forest. For example, most of Europe, including Britain, used to be covered by forests. The forests have gone because of the activities of people. Now, there is concern that similar events are taking place in the remaining large forests of the world, especially in tropical rain forests.

Forests are cleared for a number of reasons:

- **growing crops** – in some parts of the world, communities clear a small area of forested land, grow crops on it until the fertility of the soil becomes too low, then move on and repeat the process in another area of forest. The trees are usually cleared by cutting down and then burning, partly because this is the quickest and easiest way of doing it, and partly because the ash from the trees adds mineral ions to the soil. In other areas, land is cleared permanently for farming, as has happened, for example, in previous centuries in North America and Europe.

- **space for building** – the use of previously forested land for building houses, industrial plants and roads has increased as populations have increased, and as perceived needs for efficient transport and productive industry have increased.

- **wood** – wood is used for fuel, or for building houses, bridges, furniture and so on.

The effects of deforestation are wide ranging (Fig 12).

As forests are destroyed, this removes **habitats** for the animals, plants, fungi and microorganisms that live in them. Thus, **biodiversity** decreases. This is especially important in tropical rain forests, which have very high biodiversity.

Forests have an important role in the **water cycle**. When it rains, they act like giant sponges, absorbing much of the water that falls, and then gradually releasing it back into the air as water vapour through transpiration. If large areas of trees are removed, this can reduce the amount of water vapour that returns to the air, and may reduce rainfall either locally or in nearby regions.

Deciduous trees, such as oak trees, regrow from the base if they are cut down. So, to destroy a forest of deciduous trees, you have to do more than simply cut them down. You have to dig out the roots and cultivate the ground to prevent them from regrowing, or burn them. On the other hand, most conifers do not regrow after cutting down.

Removal of forests can increase **soil erosion** and the risk of **flooding**. With the trees removed, rain drops hit the soil directly, rather than falling through a canopy of leaves. The force with which the drops hit the ground – especially in tropical regions where rainfall can be very violent – dislodges soil particles and causes erosion, especially on slopes. If there are no tree roots to hold the soil, large amounts wash down the slopes into rivers. Large quantities of sediment can block these rivers, increasing the risk of flooding.

The flooding risk also increases because, when rain falls, it flows very quickly into the rivers; if there were forests, they would absorb a lot of this rain water.

Old trees have been absorbing carbon dioxide for many years. If they are burnt when they are cut down, the carbon dioxide is released all at once, and may contribute to the **enhanced greenhouse effect**.

Fig 12
Effects of deforestation

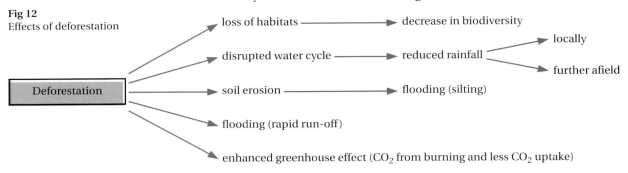

loss of habitats ——————→ decrease in biodiversity

disrupted water cycle ——————→ reduced rainfall ——→ locally / further afield

soil erosion ——————→ flooding (silting)

flooding (rapid run-off)

enhanced greenhouse effect (CO_2 from burning and less CO_2 uptake)

There is some disagreement about whether deforestation does contribute significantly to the enhanced greenhouse effect. A mature tree probably takes in almost the same amount of carbon dioxide for photosynthesis that it releases in respiration. Thus, simply removing mature trees does not have a significant effect on the carbon dioxide content of the atmosphere, especially if other plants are then grown in that area.

Sustainable management of forests involves making use of them without destroying them. It aims to maintain or increase the biodiversity within them. For example:

- if trees are to be used for timber or for making paper, then the logging company can **replant** a new tree or several trees for every one that it cuts down

- logging can be done **selectively**, so that only some trees are taken out of any one area of forest at a time, and the habitat is not completely destroyed

- deciduous trees can be **coppiced** for timber, that is they can be cut down to a base from which they are allowed to regrow for several years before being coppiced again. Different parts of the wood are coppiced each year, in rotation. A coppiced woodland is likely to have a greater biodiversity than one in which the trees are not cut down at all, because the rotational coppicing provides a range of different habitats, in which different species of plants and animals can live.

Desertification

Desertification is the conversion of fertile land into a desert. There are many definitions, but in general a desert is an area where rainfall is too low to support very much life – often the measure used is less than 500 mm rain per year. Deserts may be cold, such as the Gobi desert in Mongolia, or hot, such as the Sahara desert in northern Africa.

In many parts of the world, where rainfall is low, deserts form naturally. However, there are also many areas of **marginal land**, where rainfall is low but just enough for some crops to be grown. It is these marginal lands that are in greatest danger of becoming deserts as a result of human activity (Fig 13).

Desertification may happen as a result of the following:

Overgrazing – if people graze too many animals on an area of marginal land, then plants cannot regrow as quickly as the animals eat them. As plant cover is lost, the soil is exposed to rain and wind, and is easily eroded. (Desert soils tend to be light and thin, because they do not contain much humus.) The trampling of the animals increases this effect. In the past, many of the communities who lived on marginal lands had a nomadic lifestyle – they moved from place to place and so did not have too great an impact on any one area. Now they are more likely to settle close to a water supply that has been provided for them, or close to hospitals and other services.

Removal of trees and shrubs – people living on marginal lands harvest plant material for fuel or building. The loss of plant cover increases erosion and decreases soil fertility.

Use of marginal land for growing arable crops – cultivation of marginal land loosens the soil and increases the risk of wind or water erosion. This also often involves irrigation, which can lower the water table under the soil and so reduce the amount of water available over the long term. Also, the irrigation water usually contains significant amounts of dissolved salts. These are left in the soil as the water evaporates and can eventually become so concentrated that plants no longer grow.

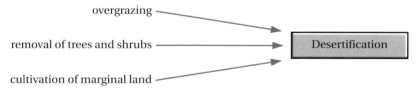

Fig 13
Causes of desertification

Acid rain

> [D] Acid rain is precipitation (usually rain, but it can also be snow) with a pH of less than about 4.5. The acidity is caused by the release of sulphur dioxide and nitrogen oxides into the atmosphere.

Rain is naturally slightly acidic with a pH of around 5.6, because carbon dioxide dissolves in it to form a weak acid.

Sulphur dioxide, SO_2, is produced when coal and – to a lesser extent – oil are burnt. Coal contains sulphur, which oxidises to form sulphur dioxide during combustion.

Significant amounts of sulphur dioxide are not released from car exhausts, because petrol and diesel do not contain much sulphur.

Nitrogen oxides such as **NO** and **NO₂** are produced when nitrogen gas from the air combines with oxygen as petrol and diesel fuels undergo combustion in car engines.

The nitrogen that forms the nitrogen oxides does not come from the fuels, but from the air that is drawn in to the engine as the fuels burn.

Sulphur dioxide and nitrogen oxides are carried high into the air, and may travel long distances. They may undergo **oxidation**, catalysed by other gases such as ozone or ammonia in the atmosphere. They react with **water** in the atmosphere, especially when this is in the form of liquid droplets in clouds. As a result, **sulphuric acid**, H_2SO_4, and nitric acid, HNO_3, are formed (Fig 14).

Acid rain has several harmful effects on living organisms.

The harmful effects of acid rain are decreased on soils which have a high pH, that is limestone soils, because limestone contains calcium carbonate which can neutralise acids.

When acid rain falls onto the soil it can **leach out mineral ions** with positive charges (cations) such as aluminium, lead, mercury and calcium. These ions are washed into waterways, where they may cause harm to aquatic organisms. For example, aluminium ions affect the gills of young fish. Lead and mercury are toxic to many organisms, because they act as non-active site-directed enzyme inhibitors.

The low pH of water in streams and lakes affected by acid rain may reduce the production or activity of **enzymes** in organisms such as fish.

Acid rain is **harmful to trees** and other plants. Conifers grow poorly in areas where rain is acidic. The exact way in which acid rain causes these problems is not clear, but it probably affects the ability of the roots to absorb minerals from the soil, and weakens the trees so that they are less able to withstand other stresses such as drought.

Fig 14
Causes of acid rain

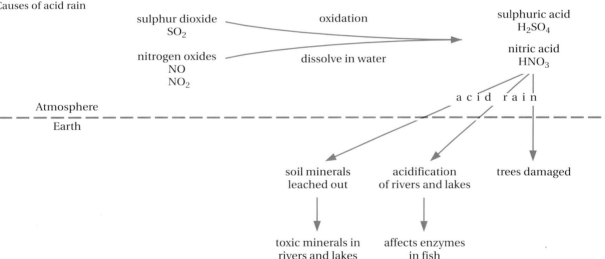

The enhanced greenhouse effect

Short-wave radiation from the Sun passes down through the Earth's atmosphere and is reflected back from the ground as long-wave radiation (Fig 15). Atmospheric gases such as **carbon dioxide** and **methane** absorb this long-wave radiation, stopping much of it from leaving the Earth. This helps to keep the temperature of the Earth much higher than it would otherwise be. The warming effect of these gases is called the **greenhouse effect**, and the gases are sometimes called **greenhouse gases**.

It is important to realise that we need the greenhouse effect. Without it the Earth would be too cold to support life.

In recent years, the concentrations of carbon dioxide and methane in the atmosphere have been rising, and so more long-wave radiation is being

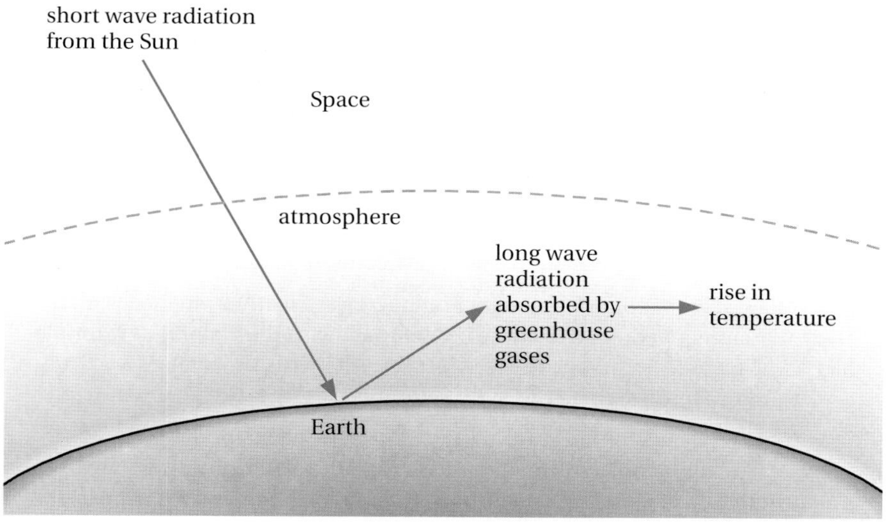

Fig 15
The greenhouse effect

short wave radiation from the Sun

Space

atmosphere

long wave radiation absorbed by greenhouse gases → rise in temperature

Earth

trapped. This is called the **enhanced greenhouse effect**, and there is evidence that it is causing an increase in average temperatures on Earth. This is **global warming**. Although we cannot be sure exactly what is causing the temperature rise, it does seem to be at least partly due to the increased release of carbon dioxide from the burning of fossil fuels.

It is extremely difficult to predict how great a problem global warming will be. This is because we still do not fully understand the rate at which greenhouse gases such as carbon dioxide are entering and leaving the atmosphere, so it is impossible to predict with any precision what will happen to the levels of these gases in the future. For example, we still do not understand how quickly the oceans might absorb 'extra' carbon dioxide from the atmosphere; nor do we know how great an effect deforestation might have on carbon dioxide levels.

Although many attempts have been made to model the possible effects of a global temperature rise, there are so many variables involved that the best that can be done is to provide a range of possibilities. For example, although everyone agrees that weather patterns will change, different models produce different predictions for what might happen in particular areas.

If average temperatures do rise more than a degree or so, then the following events will probably happen.

Ice sheets will melt even faster than they are doing at present, so sea levels will rise and low-lying land will be flooded. Whole countries, such as Bangladesh and the Maldives, could disappear.

Ocean currents, which are caused by temperature gradients in the atmosphere and the seas, could change their courses. For example, the Gulf Stream that flows north-eastwards across the Atlantic and brings warm waters to the coast of the United Kingdom, could flow in a different direction. This would cause a significant cooling in the climate of the UK.

Raw sewage

Sewage is liquid waste that flows from homes and industries. It consists of water in which urine, faeces, detergents and other chemicals are carried. Most sewage flows to sewage treatment works, where filtration and the action of bacteria break down these substances, producing a clean **effluent** that can be released safely into waterways. However, in some places this does not happen, and untreated or **raw sewage** is allowed to flow into rivers or the sea.

Raw sewage can cause a number of problems.

Raw sewage contains **viruses** and **bacteria**, mostly from faeces, that can infect people who come into contact with the water. For example, the bacterium that causes **cholera** and the virus that causes **poliomyelitis** can be transmitted in this way.

Raw sewage contains organic nutrients that can support large populations of **bacteria**. These bacteria respire aerobically. They therefore use up large quantities of oxygen from the water, so that the water is said to have a high **biochemical oxygen demand**, or **BOD**. As the bacteria use up the oxygen, there is less available for other organisms such as invertebrates or fish. These are either killed by the lack of oxygen, or they leave the area. The water becomes populated by organisms that can survive in low oxygen environments, such as *Chironomus* and *Tubifex* (see Unit 2 page 36). There are relatively few species that can survive in such conditions, so **biodiversity** decreases. This process, in which an input of nutrients causes a drop in oxygen availability and thus a change in the community, is called **eutrophication**.

Raw sewage often contains high concentrations of **suspended particles**, which make the water cloudy. Light cannot penetrate, so aquatic plants cannot photosynthesise. They die, providing yet more food for bacteria and so increasing eutrophication.

Raw sewage may contain **toxic substances** such as heavy metals from industry and oestrogens (female hormones) from urine. Heavy metals act as non-active site-directed inhibitors of enzymes, and so are very toxic to aquatic organisms. Oestrogens may cause hormonal imbalances in fish and invertebrates, resulting in changes such as feminisation (the development of female characteristics in male animals).

Fertilisers

D

*Fertilisers are chemicals that are applied to the land on which crops are grown in order to supply nutrients to the plants. They may be **organic** (such as manure) or **inorganic** (such as ammonium nitrate).*

Both **organic** and **inorganic** fertilisers can enter waterways if they **leach** from the soil and are washed into the ground water. This is most likely to happen if:

- too much fertiliser is applied, so that the plants cannot absorb it all

- fertiliser is applied at a time when plants are not growing actively

- application is carried out when rain is expected, or very close to a waterway.

The components of fertilisers that cause most pollution problems are **nitrate** and **phosphate** ions. In general, nitrate causes more problems than phosphate because it is more soluble. However, phosphate can cause more long-lasting problems, because it becomes trapped in sediment at the bottom of waterways. Both nitrate and phosphate can cause **eutrophication**. This happens because the addition of these mineral ions to the water can increase the growth of **algae**. This is called an **algal bloom**. Other aquatic plants cannot compete successfully for light with the large algal population, and so they die. The algae also die eventually. This provides extra nutrients for the eutrophication-causing aerobic bacteria, as explained above.

European legislation

There is a great deal of legislation produced by the UK government and by the European Union which attempts to regulate activities that might cause pollution.

You do not need to know details of any particular rules and regulations, but you should have some awareness of the *kind* of laws that are in force and also be prepared to comment on the possible effects of any specific laws that are described in examination questions.

A good place to find information about current environmental issues, including legislation, is on the Internet. Try these three sites to start with:

- the UK Environment Agency site at http://www.environment-agency.gov.uk

- the European Environmental Law site at http://www.eel.nl

- the European Environment Agency site at http://www.eea.eu.int/

In general, farmers avoid the risk of pollution by fertilisers. Most farmers do not want to cause water pollution and it is not in their interest to spend large amounts of money buying and applying fertilisers that are just washed away.

Phosphates are found in some detergents, so they may be present in raw sewage.

Remember that the reduction in oxygen supply is caused by the *aerobic bacteria*, and not by the increased population of plants.

AS3 Energy and the environment Sample unit test

1. The diagram below shows an organism of the genus *Rhizopus*.

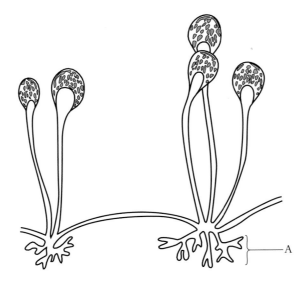

(a)   Describe the role of part **A** in the nutrition of the organism.

....

....

....

(2 marks)

(b)   Explain how parasitic nutrition differs from the nutrition of *Rhizopus*.

....

....

....

(2 marks)

(c)   Describe the roles of organisms such as *Rhizopus* in the cycling of carbon within an
ecosystem.

....

....

....

(3 marks)

(Total 7 marks)

AS3 Energy and the environment Sample unit test

2. *(a)* The table below shows mean values for primary productivity for four ecosystems: temperate deciduous forest, tropical forest, temperate grassland, and intensively cultivated land in a temperate region.

Ecosystem	Primary productivity (kJ m $^{-2}$ yr $^{-1}$)
temperate deciduous forest	26 000
tropical forest	40 000
temperate grassland	15 000
intensively cultivated land in temperate region	30 000

(i) Suggest *two* reasons to account for the higher primary productivity of a tropical forest compared with a temperate forest.

1 ....

....

2 ....

....

(2 marks)

(ii) Suggest explanations for the difference in primary productivity between temperate grassland and intensively cultivated land.

....

....

....

....

(3 marks)

(b)   Describe how you would estimate the fresh biomass of the producers in a grassland ecosystem.

....

....

....

....

....

(4 marks)

(c)   Suggest why productivity of an ecosystem is measured in units of energy rather than units of biomass.

....

....

....

(2 marks)

(Total 11 marks)

3. Study the passage and data below and then answer the questions that follow.

Pollution of freshwater ecosystems

The pollution of fresh water is of concern for environmental reasons, and also because it has implications for human health if used as a source of drinking water. Pollutants include inorganic ions such as nitrate, NO_3^-, and phosphate, PO_4^{3-}, organic substances such as PCBs, and pathogenic microorganisms such as coliform bacteria.

The addition of nitrate to rivers and lakes can cause eutrophication. The major source of nitrates in rivers in western Europe is run-off from agricultural land. High levels of nitrate in the water courses in some areas give particular concern, and the EC Nitrate Directive (91/676/EEC) requires that pollution in these areas is tackled by the governments of each member state. In the UK, 68 Nitrate Vulnerable Zones (NVZs) have been designated, and all farmers in these areas must comply with strict legislation designed to reduce the amount of nitrate that they release into the environment.

Polychlorinated biphenols (PCBs) are now banned in the UK, but are still widely used in a variety of industrial contexts in other parts of the world. They are fat soluble and highly toxic, and remain in the environment for long periods. They show bioaccumulation, increasing in concentration in the tissues of organisms towards the end of a food chain.

Water for drinking is sometimes taken from underground aquifers and sometimes from rivers. It is always treated before release into the public supply system, and strict quality standards are laid down to which the water supply companies must comply. Water authorities take regular samples to ensure that these standards are being met.

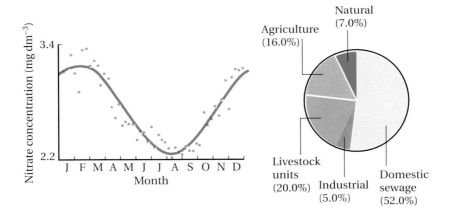

Figure 1 Means of weekly nitrate concentrations in a river in south-west England from 1965 to 1975

Figure 2 The relative contributions of different sources to phosphates in rivers in the United Kingdom

Table 1 Results of samples taken by a UK water company throughout one year

Key

FC = faecal coliforms, which come from human and animal guts

TC = total coliforms, including those which are naturally present in the environment

Point of sampling	Number of samples taken	Percentage of samples containing coliforms	
water leaving treatment works	15 835	FC	0.00
		TC	0.06
water in service reservoirs	20 888	FC	0.03
		TC	0.19
water at customer tap	10 535	FC	0.04
		TC	0.31

(a) Explain how the addition of nitrate to a river can cause eutrophication.

....

....

....

....

....

....

(5 marks)

(b) Suggest how each of the following rules, which must be followed on farms in NVZs, can help to reduce nitrate pollution of waterways.

(i) Do not apply nitrogen fertiliser between 1 September and 1 February.

....

....

....

(3 marks)

(ii) All farmers must keep records relating to livestock numbers and the use of inorganic nitrogen fertiliser and organic manures on their land.

....

....

....

(2 marks)

(c) Suggest why no legislation equivalent to that for NVZs has been applied to farmers regarding pollution by phosphates.

....

....

(2 marks)

(d) Explain why bioaccumulation occurs with PCBs but not with nitrates or phosphates.

....

....

....

....

....

(3 marks)

(e) (i) Name *one* disease which is caused by bacteria that can be transmitted in water.

....

(1 mark)

(ii) Describe the changes in the number of coliforms in water between leaving the water treatment works and flowing out of a customer's tap, and suggest reasons for these changes.

....

....

....

....

....

....

....

(4 marks)

(Total 20 marks)

Unit test answers

Each point that ends with a semicolon is worth one mark. The sign / indicates alternative answers, either of which will gain you the mark. Where '3 max' appears, this means that any 3 of the marking points will gain you the maximum 3 marks available. Half marks are never awarded. You either get a complete mark or none at all.

1 (a) penetration of / anchorage in substrate / food source ;
    secretes enzymes ;
    absorption   2 max
  (b) nutrients already soluble / no need for digestion ;
    source of nutrients is a living organism ;
    detrimental effect on host ;
    Rhizopus is a saprobiont / feeds on dead or decaying matter   2 max
  (c) use organic carbon compounds in dead / decaying matter ;
    in respiration ;
    release carbon dioxide   3

2 (a) (i) higher / constant temperature / little seasonal change ;
      higher plant density ;
      higher water availability ;
      temperate trees lose leaves for part of year ;
      more light / higher light intensity   2 max
   (ii) crops all same type of plant / monoculture ;
      use of crop rotation / fertilisers applied / irrigation ;
      pests / diseases controlled ;
      crop varieties selected for high yield ;
      replanting after harvest   3 max
  (b) take several / random samples ;
    use of quadrat / sample of stated area ;
    remove plants / count number of plants ;
    remove all consumers ;
    weigh to find fresh mass / weigh one and multiply by number of plants ;
    multiply by area of grassland   4 max
  (c) biomass includes inorganic component ;
    same biomass of different organisms has different energy content ;
    productivity in energy units is true reflection of energy captured   2 max

3 (a) nitrate increases plant / algal growth ;
    plants / algae die ;
    so bacterial population increases as they feed on them ;
    bacteria respire aerobically ;
    reduce oxygen content / increase BOD ;
    aerobic organisms / fish / invertebrates die or leave area   5 max
  (b)(i) more rainfall then / more likelihood of leaching ;
      less plant cover / plants not growing ;
      so plants will not take up nitrate ;
      reference to nitrate concentration data in Figure 1   3 max

   (ii) ensure nitrate added to land does not exceed its requirements ;
      to ensure compliance with legislation ;
      to help authorities to check on and remedy possible sources of nitrate in waterways
                                               2 max
  (c) Figure 2 shows that farming is not the major source of phosphates in rivers ;
    most phosphate comes from domestic sewage ;
    perhaps phosphate is less important than nitrate as a pollutant   2 max
  (d) PCBs are fat soluble, nitrate and phosphate are not ;
    nitrate and phosphate are converted into other substances by living organisms but PCBs are not converted to anything else / PCBs not biodegradable ;
    so PCBs accumulate in tissues, nitrate and phosphate do not ;
    one consumer eats many producers / one carnivore eats many herbivores   3 max
  (e) (i) cholera / typhoid / other suitable   1
   (ii) numbers of both FCs and TCs increase steadily between treatment works and tap ;
      water treatment completely destroys all FCs but not TCs ;
      TCs increase more than FCs ;
      manipulation of figures to support argument ;
      faecal coliforms enter water in reservoirs from livestock / pets / people ;
      sensible suggestion about how TCs enter from general environment   4 max